WARRIORS, TOMBS AND TEMPLES:
CHINA'S ENDURING LEGACY

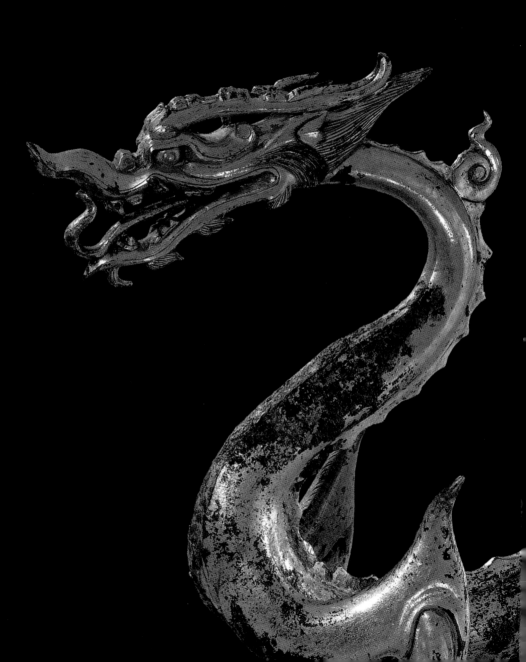

WARRIORS, TOMBS AND TEMPLES: CHINA'S ENDURING LEGACY

The Guide to the Exhibition

By

Suzanne E. Cahill

Bowers Museum, Santa Ana, California
Houston Museum of Natural Science, Houston, Texas

This guide was published on the occasion of the exhibition *Warriors, Tombs and Temples: China's Enduring Legacy.* The exclusive one-year tour was held at Bowers Museum, Santa Ana, California from October 1, 2011 to March 4, 2012 and at Houston Museum of Natural Science, Houston, Texas from April 1 to September 3, 2012.

ISBN: 978-0-615-51397-3

Exhibition Organized by:
Bowers Museum
2002 N. Main St.
Santa Ana, California, 92706 USA
www.bowers.org

Houston Museum of Natural Science
5555 Hermann Park Drive
Houston, Texas 77030 USA
www.hmns.org

Photography © Wang da Gang
with the permission of the State Administration of Cultural Heritage and the Shaanxi Provincial Cultural Relics Bureau
Designed and Printed in Shanghai

PREVIOUS PAGE: **Gilded dragon.**

FOLLOWING PAGE: **Gold ornament in the shape of a tree.**

GUIDE CONTENTS

DEDICATED

TO

MARY AND JOHN TU

FOR THEIR WARM FRIENDSHIP AND
GENEROUS SUPPORT OF THIS EXHIBITION
AND THE BOWERS MUSEUM

WARRIORS, TOMBS AND TEMPLES

This publication serves as a guide to the exhibition *Warriors, Tombs and Temples: China's Enduring Legacy.* The objects within are drawn from three of the greatest and most important periods of Chinese history, the Qin (221 – 206 BCE), Han (206 BCE – 220 CE), and Tang (618 – 907 CE) Dynasties. Covering 1100 years, these eras are characterized by unification, standardization, control of vast territory, great wealth, and foundational institution-building in the areas of government, family, and religion. The Han and Tang in particular were high points of culture and technology, looked back to with pride by Chinese people and admired by others all over the world today.

The exhibition draws on some of the most important excavations from the burial complexes of emperors, the tombs of royal family members, tombs of elite individuals, and the magnificent deposits placed into the Famen monastery treasure crypt. All of these sites are found in and around the modern city of Xi'an, the location of the capital cities of all three dynasties. Much of the material has never been exhibited or has rarely before been seen in the United States. The objects are not only beautiful and striking, but they also tell stories and supply information about many important aspects of life and values in early and medieval China. For example, they tell us about the daily and ritual lives of the elites, including the royal families, of each era. Along with what elites wore, rode on, ate from, and took to their tombs, the objects reveal tensions, controversies, and plots at court. Almost all of the Qin material and much of the Han and Tang material comes from royal tombs.

The objects also tell us about daily life in the capital cities: how people made a living, worshipped, traded, and buried their dead.

Objects such as the terra cotta warriors from the Qin and Han Dynasties and the spectacular Tang metalwork, tell us how they were made: we can trace the technologies of craft production, workshop practices, and government regulations on crafts, as well as changes and continuity in craft production and style over this long period. Other objects disclose beliefs and values concerning family and gender, and the social systems and practices related to those beliefs. They also embody beliefs about life after death, relations between the living and the dead, and funerary beliefs and practices. The objects change over time, reflecting changes in these beliefs.

Many of the objects, beginning in the Han and increasing in the Tang period, reflect the influence of trade along the Silk Road on Chinese art and culture. Such things as Buddhism, horses, polo, and new forms of metal working enter China from the west via these important trade routes. The objects from the Famen monastery provide information about Buddhist beliefs and practices, and how these were folded into the daily life and material culture of elites and commoners alike.

The images on the following pages are dramatic enough to appeal to anyone of any age group or level of familiarity with Chinese culture. And the stories the pieces tell are so vivid that the reader will gain an increased awareness of China's great historical traditions and its importance in the world today.

ABOVE: **View of Han Emperor Jingdi's burial mound.**

THE QIN DYNASTY (221 – 206 BCE)

The Qin Dynasty arose in the culturally unpromising but strategically well-located state of the same name in northwest China. By the Warring States era (450 – 221 BCE), agrarian reforms, efficient administration, military preparedness, superior weaponry, willingness to employ aliens, and eagerness to experiment with new ideas gave the Qin state advantages over its rivals.

Then a brilliant, charismatic, and ruthless ruler, King Zheng, took the Qin throne in 259 BCE. Ruling his kingdom with strong central control, strict laws, and an emphasis on agriculture and the military, King Zheng led his small state in battle after battle to decisive military victories over all the other states within a few short decades. Once in power, he declared the inauguration of the Qin Dynasty and bestowed upon himself the grandiose title of Qin Shihuangdi, literally "the First Divine Emperor of the Qin Dynasty." (He is also known as Qin Shi Huang.)

His government put into place a centralized imperial bureaucracy and standardized weights, measures, currency, roads, and the writing system. He began a massive infrastructure campaign and demolished the walls dividing the former warring states while joining up old sections of the Great Wall to create a symbolic boundary to the north. At the same time as he was building his capital city of Xianyang with its palaces, he also constructed his tomb, a massive mound just outside the capital, guarded by terra cotta soldiers in satellite pits.

LEFT:
View of front lines of Qin Shihuangdi's terra cotta army.

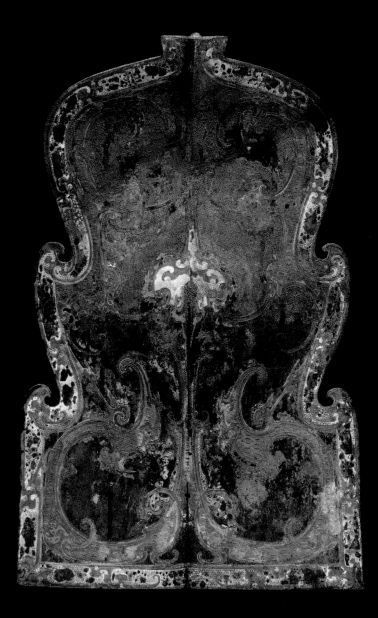

COLLAPSE OF THE QIN DYNASTY

The Qin Empire did not long survive Qin Shihuangdi. He died in 210 BCE. Soon afterward, a combination of factors led to the overthrow of his short (15 year) dynasty and the rise of the Han. These factors included overuse of human and natural resources, lack of a competent heir, and failure to establish a lasting set of civil government institutions to replace the military means by which he won his victories.

LEFT:
**Bronze shield found with bronze
chariot and horses on the side of Qin
Shihuangdi's funerary mound.**

LEFT:
Armored military officer. His hands once held a long-handled weapon.

THE TERRA COTTA ARMY OF QIN SHIHUANGDI

The terra cotta army represented the honor guard of the emperor and was located to the east of his mausoleum, the direction from which an attack might be expected. It was composed of infantry armed with crossbows and long-handled weapons, cavalrymen, and chariots, all in battle formation. More than 1,000 such figures have been excavated from what has been named Pit 1, and the estimate is that there are another 6,000 yet to be recovered. The realism of these life-size figures and their sheer numbers have earned the terra cotta army the title of eighth wonder of the ancient world.

Adjacent to the army in nearby Pit 2, a total of 160 kneeling archers was uncovered. The presence of some swords nearby may indicate that these men were also prepared for hand-to-hand fighting, thus explaining their armor. The realistic twisted and kneeling posture demonstrates the high level of artistry achieved by the craftsmen of the Qin period.

LEFT:
Figure of a kneeling archer. This is the only warrior found to date with a green face. It is a subject of debate among scholars.

PREVIOUS PAGES:
Life-size chariot horse unearthed from Pit 1 of Qin Shihuangdi's tomb compound.

ABOVE:
Bronze sword with a surface that appears to have undergone a treatment to prevent corrosion; the achievement is considered remarkable at such an early date.

THE HAN DYNASTY (206 BCE – 220 CE)

The Han Dynasty began with Liu Bang, known in historical records as Emperor Gaozu (or Gaodi), one of the great heroes of Chinese history. Born a peasant who turned bandit and then rebel, he vanquished the last Qin ruler, defeated his own rivals, and founded the Han Dynasty. Gaozu made his capital city at Chang'an, near the ruins of Xianyang, quickly unified the empire, and established administrative institutions that created a stable and centralized empire lasting more than 400 years.

Although the rhetoric of the Han rulers and historians strongly distinguished the Han from the Qin, whom they characterized as cruel and rapacious, in fact the Han inherited and built upon Qin unification, standardization, and institutions. The Han system of imperial bureaucracy, at its most effective, met the challenges of administering a huge, diverse empire.

The Han Dynasty also saw the first great opening of the Silk Road: routes of trade and communication leading from China across Central Asia to Persia, India, and eventually to the Mediterranean. Han expansion ushered in a new era of contact with other peoples that included trade, war, diplomacy, and exchange of technology and belief systems. Not coincidentally, the Han was a period of enormous technological and scientific progress that included the invention of the compass and paper and the mining of coal for use as fuel.

LEFT:
Partially excavated terra cotta army of Han emperor Jingdi.

THE TERRA COTTA WARRIORS OF HAN EMPEROR GAOZU

Two groups of warriors, one of standing infantry and the other of mounted cavalry soldiers, were excavated from the tomb compound of the founder of the Han Dynasty, Liu Bang, known after his death as Gaozu or Gaodi. The similarities between the Qin terra cotta army and this group are striking: the terra cotta figures assembled as armies in military formation, including cavalry and infantry, suggest both preparation for war and a funeral procession.

LEFT:
**Detail of mounted cavalry soldier from
Gaozu's tomb compound.**

RIGHT:
Mounted cavalry soldier and horse.

FOLLOWING PAGES:
Standing infantry soldier with shield.

The two groups of standing infantry and mounted cavalry soldiers warriors come from royally sponsored satellite tombs, dated 171 – 141 BCE, perhaps those of the important military generals and high officials, Zhou Po (d. 169 BCE) and his son Zhou Yafu (d. 147 BCE). The soldiers, arranged in neat formations, hold shields and wear armor. In the Han Dynasty when an important military official died, the imperial court gave him an elaborate funeral, using military formations in the funeral procession.

ABOVE:
Detail of infantry soldier's painted armor and quiver.

RIGHT:
Standing infantry soldier with shield. The similarity to Qin shields is clear.

THE TERRA COTTA WARRIORS OF HAN EMPEROR JINGDI

The fifth Han emperor, Jingdi (r. 180 – 157 BCE), was considered a paragon of effective rule, personal frugality, and Confucian virtue. His reign was a period of order, strong central government, and stability. His tomb compound is located north of the Wei River in a line of Han imperial tombs. A complex just south of Jingdi's burial mound is more than five times larger than that of the Qin terra cotta warriors. Twenty-four pits there contained more than 40,000 clay figures, one-third life size. Their smiling faces contrast with the sterner features of the Qin soldiers. These soldiers originally had movable arms and wore silk and hemp clothing.

Although numerous, the Han figures are much smaller than the Qin warriors, suggesting that the Han rulers symbolically demonstrated restraint and frugality by using limited material in contrast to the extravagance and waste of the Qin.

RIGHT:
Figure of a striding warrior. His wooden arms have long since disintegrated.

FOLLOWING PAGES:
Cavalry soldiers, uniquely formed to fit atop a horse.

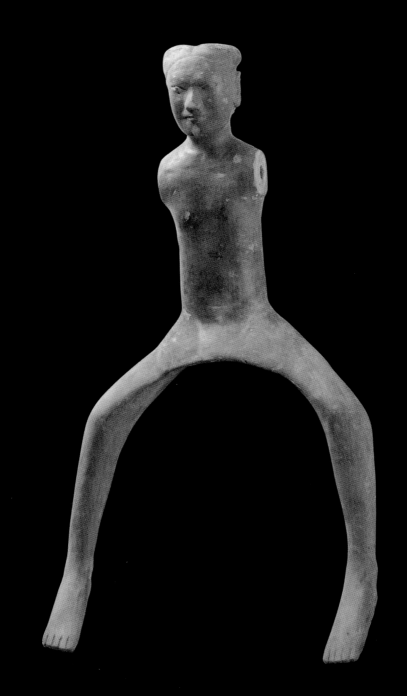

LEFT:
Impressions from the textiles once worn by this armored warrior and his painted face are clearly visible.

DOMESTIC GOODS FOR THE AFTERLIFE

Goods unearthed from tombs are indications of what daily life was like for people from various social classes in and around capital cities. Surviving Chinese texts focus on urban life and mostly ignore the countryside, but tomb furnishings give insight to a rich array of domestic animals, farm implements and rural buildings.

LEFT:
Model of a two-story rural building.

The objects and figures recovered from the Yangling cemetery of the Han emperor Jingdi paint a picture of a peaceful and prosperous agricultural economy.

ABOVE:
Figure of a sow.

Among those excavated were domestic animals, agricultural machinery, carts and tools, weights and measures, weapons, and storage jars filled with real grain.

ABOVE:
Figure of a sheep.

FOLLOWING PAGES:
Hundreds of horses, dogs, goats, sheep and swine figures unearthed at Emperor Jingdi's burial complex.

ELABORATE TOMB ENTRANCE FOR AN ELITE PERSON

This doorframe and doors show the architectural context of tomb art. Tomb architecture imitates vernacular building architecture, supporting the argument that the tomb was intended as a dwelling place for the dead. The images on the doorframe represent both mythical beings and human activities. Mythical beings such as this monster served as tomb guardians that protected the occupant from evil spirits while the depictions of human activities symbolized the life of the occupant as well as the events that occurred during the burial ceremony.

RIGHT:
Door detail from the tomb of a member of the elite showing the protective mask of a mythical monster.

FOLLOWING PAGES:
Tomb doors and doorframe with scenes from life and myths.

THE TANG DYNASTY (618 – 907 CE)

The Tang Dynasty, as countless flattering modern movies and television dramas attest, has captured the imagination of modern Chinese people who look back upon the period with pride and enthusiasm. With a succession of effective emperors on the throne, a huge economy, and vast territory, Tang China experienced a great age of prosperity and international prestige. For much of this era, government power rested on a secure tax base of agriculture and trade, a well-organized bureaucracy ran the country, a mighty and well-equipped military kept peace along ever-expanding borders, and ordinary subjects of the emperor enjoyed a relatively high quality of life. Historians consider the Tang era the golden age of poetry, the arts, and sciences. Daoism and Buddhism matured and flourished, becoming part of the cultural and geographic landscape. Contact with Westerners along the Silk Road increased, and Chinese interest in the West, the exotic occident, grew. Foreign elements increasingly influenced Chinese material culture, especially enriching the ancient Chinese technologies of metallurgy and textile production.

RIGHT:
Headdress of gold, silver, pearls, jade and other semi-precious stones unearthed from the tomb of an elite family.

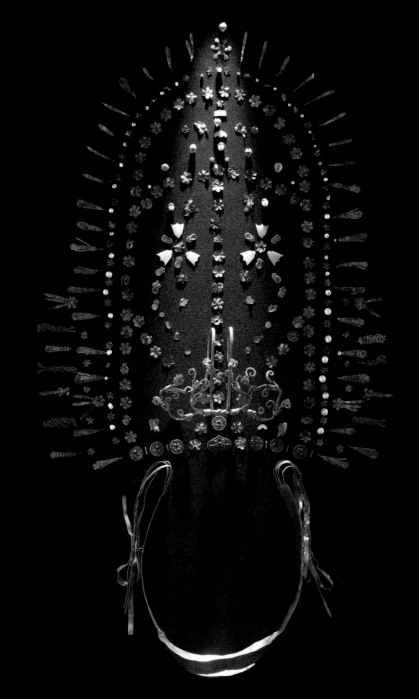

IDEALS OF TANG BEAUTY

Female figures were intended as companions and servants for the tomb occupant in the afterlife. The Tang figures are especially interesting, closely tracking changes in fashion in dress, hairstyle, and makeup throughout the era. Early in the Tang period, female figures are slender. They engage in a range of activities such as polo playing and hunting, suggesting the relative freedom women were allowed during this era, probably under the influence of the cultures of their semi-nomadic neighbors to the west. By the mid-eighth century, the ideal of female beauty begins to change and the statues favor more full-figured women in static poses. People often say that the stouter figures reflect the appearance of the ideal female beauty Yang Guifei (d. 756), consort of the Tang emperor Xuanzong (r. 712 – 756), but there is no reliable evidence either that she was portly or that the figures copy her in any way.

LEFT:
Female attendant recovered from Prince Li Xian's tomb.

GILDED DRAGON

The dragon, symbol of the emperor and especially of the Tang emperor Xuanzong (r. 712 – 756) who was supposed to be a reincarnated dragon, was ubiquitous in Tang art. Several such figures have been excavated in or near Tang palace grounds. The dragon is a powerful and mostly benevolent creature in Chinese mythology, the bringer of rain and the symbol of springtime and life. From the end of the Han through the Tang period, the dragon was also associated with Daoism and the search for immortality; dragons were favored mounts of Daoist transcendents and deities. Examples of the slender striding or standing dragon, with its long snout, curling tongue, single horn, scales, and sinuous tail go back to the Northern Wei period (386 – 534 CE). This lithe and nimble figure is a particularly fine example of the metalworker's art.

RIGHT:
Gilded dragon with iron core.

FINE CHINESE METALLURGY

This miniature tree worked in filigree on gold sheet was originally one of a set of nine unearthed, probably from a tomb, during airport construction in 1971. Despite its small scale, the tree is depicted in considerable detail, with leaves arranged in rosettes, and a vine winding around its trunk. It was originally inlaid with semiprecious stones representing fruits or flowers. It probably served as an appliqué decorating a wooden or lacquered box. The form of the tree resembles depictions of the *bodhi* tree seen behind the Buddha in paintings and sculpture during the Tang Dynasty. The *bodhi* tree is a kind of fig tree; the word means "enlightenment or awakening" in Sanskrit; this is the type of tree under which the Buddha sat in meditation until he achieved enlightenment. Trees are a constant motif in Tang art, both Buddhist and secular. The filigree, inlay, and incising on this tree remind us that the Tang was a great period for Chinese metallurgy. Metalwork of the era was deeply influenced by foreign, especially Persian, techniques.

LEFT:
Gold ornament in the shape of a tree.

RIGHT:
**Clay vessel shaped like a Buddhist stupa from
the royal tomb of the Jiemin ("Measured and
Brilliant") Heir Apparent, Prince Li Chongjun.**

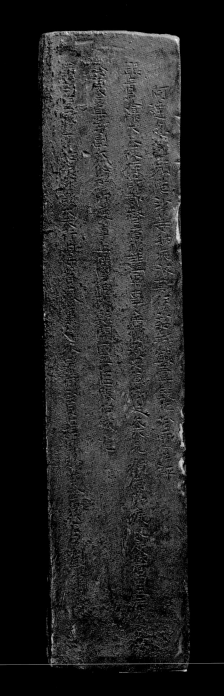

LEFT:
This jade condolence tablet is from the tomb of Heir Apparent, Prince Li Chongjun. Condolence texts were a part of the burial rites of the deceased and constituted ritual records of the funeral and the deceased.

GUARDIANS OF THE TOMB

Tomb guardians, literally "tomb settlers," are meant to protect the tomb occupant from all harm or challenges, both natural and supernatural. They may also be intended to keep the dead "settled" in the tomb so his ghost will not roam and harm his descendents. These figures were relatively numerous in tombs from the Tang Dynasty. The intriguing human and animal faces place the creatures among a large group of mythical hybrids, some benevolent and others not, that populate early Chinese art and literature.

RIGHT:
**Figure of a tomb guardian with a mustached
human face.**

LEFT:
Tomb guardian in the form of a mythical beast.

ABOVE:
Gold and rock crystal garment clasps, from the tomb of a member of the elite.

THE SPORT FOR TANG ROYALS

Polo was a favorite subject of the murals in Tang royal male tombs. Earthenware figures of both male and female polo players have frequently been found in elite burials. Polo was a huge fad at court and in the capital city, Chang'an. The Tang royal princes played and there were even teams of female players. For a while in the early Tang, the custom of drunken midnight polo games in celebration of the candidates who had passed the imperial exams caused so many casualties of China's best and brightest that they were outlawed. (The exam was one of the pathways, later the main

pathway, to high position in the government and to the wealth and prestige that came with that position.) Polo was probably a Persian import, part of the general wave of foreign influence during the first half of the Tang. The influence affected all sectors of life: fashion, food, music, and technology.

ABOVE:
Mural of two polo players, from the tomb of Prince Li Yong.

THE ROYAL HOARD OF HEJIACUN

A hoard, consisting of some two hundred and seventy objects, including pieces of metalwork of the highest quality, was excavated in 1971 at Hejia village in the southern suburbs of Xi'an. The hoard was unearthed just three blocks south of the Tang imperial palace, from the site of residence of Li Shouli, Prince of Bin and grandson of the Emperor Gaozong. The objects date to the period from 714 to 755. They were probably buried by someone, perhaps even the prince himself, fleeing from the capital during the An Lushan Rebellion (756–763).

RIGHT:
Box with decoration of Mandarin duck on lid from the possible royal hoard buried during the An Lushan Rebellion.

FOLLOWING PAGES:
Two views of a fine bowl decorated with flowers and birds.

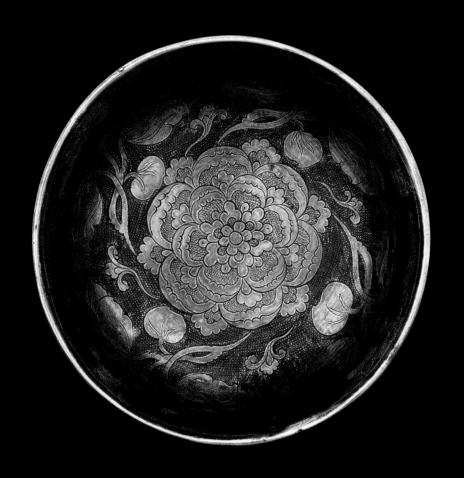

RIGHT:
**Gilt silver lock with incised
geometric decorations, from
the possible royal hoard buried
during the An Lushan Rebellion.**

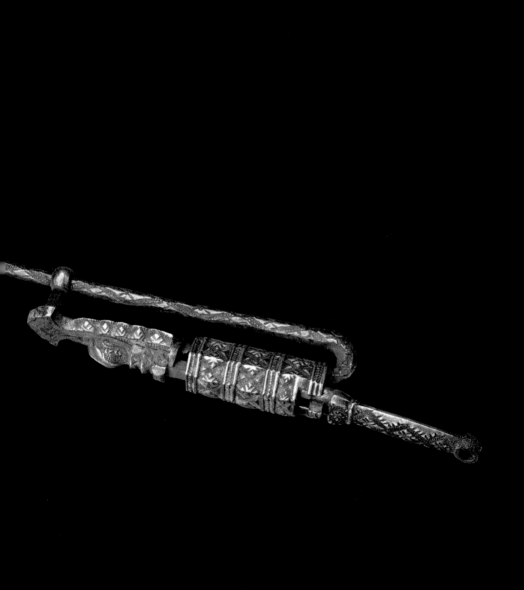

THE MEDICINE BUDDHA

This is a standard early Tang image of the Medicine Buddha, one of the cosmic Buddhas that appeared after the development of Mahayana ("greater vehicle") Buddhism, the only kind of Buddhism that took root in China.

The medicine Buddha was known for fulfilling the wishes of the devout. He especially governs matters of health. He is recognizable as a Buddha, rather than a lesser figure, by his rounded topknot, elongated earlobes, monastic robes, and lack of jewelry of any kind. His figure is more robust than Buddha figures of earlier eras. He sits on a lotus throne, a symbol of his purity, since the lotus has its roots in the mud and filth of the world but grows up above the surface of the water and only then opens and blooms. He sits lotus-style, with his legs crossed, a standard pose for Buddha figures. Representations of the Buddha changed very slowly as they were icons (holy images intended for worship or contemplation) and it was more important for the artist to depict the central figure correctly than to express individual creativity. The icon's spiritual effectiveness depended on its accurate portrayal of the deity.

LEFT:
Seated sculpture of Medicine Buddha.

FOLLOWING PAGES:
Buddhist amulets with images in relief.

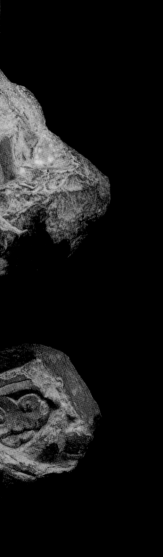

THE TREASURE-CRYPT OF FAMEN TEMPLE

Located 110 kilometers west of modern Xi'an, Famen ("Gateway to the Dharma") Temple is also known as the Famen Monastery. Buddhists consecrated a new monastery or temple with the burial of a foundation deposit of holy items, and Famen Temple was no exception. As part of its foundation deposit, the Famen Temple housed an important relic (*sarira*) of the historical Buddha in the form of a finger bone. The relic and other objects from this temple were found in a single treasure-crypt buried under the famous four-story wooden pagoda.

Famen Temple became especially prominent in the Tang Dynasty through its association with seven emperors, including Wu Zhao, the only female emperor of China. Tang rulers opened the crypt seven times (631, 660, 704, 760, 790, 819, and 873-4) to venerate the relics. On each of those occasions a huge, imperially sponsored festival to honor the relic took place, consisting of a procession of the relics to Chang'an with much pomp and circumstance and a holiday for people along the route and in the city.

LEFT:

Architectural detail of dragon's head from Famen Temple.

ABOVE:
Pure gold reliquary in the shape of a casket.

RIGHT:
Gilt silver soup bowl with lid and lotus leaf base.

ABOVE:
Yellow glass vase with appliqué decoration.

RIGHT:
Blue glass plate with floral design.

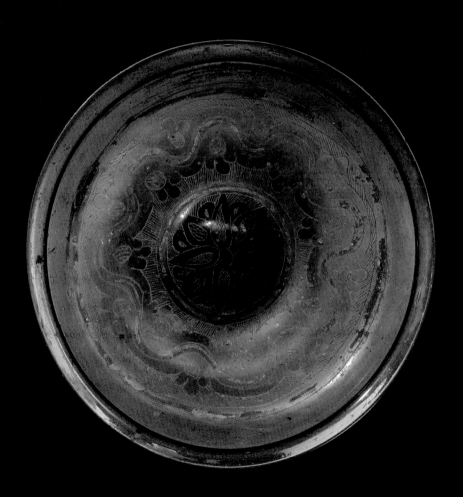

RIGHT:
**Pure gold alms bowl for
welcoming relics.**

SACRED RELIQUARY

This is one of the earliest surviving items placed into the crypt at the Gateway to the Dharma Monastery (Famen Temple), probably donated by Wu Zhao (or Wu Zetian), the only female emperor in Chinese history (r. 690 – 705). One of a series of four nesting containers, it is a reliquary in the shape of a miniature crystal sarcophagus, with nuggets of gold and lapis lazuli set into the roof. A reliquary is a container for relics (*sarira*), in this case a finger bone of the historical Buddha, Shakyamuni (566 – 486 BCE).

LEFT:
Crystal reliquary with semiprecious stones in the shape of a sarcophagus.

The crystal reliquary was found inside a gilt silver casket dedicated by Emperor Yizong in 871 in preparation for a great Buddhist festival that took place in 873, when he and his son Xizong removed the finger bone relic from the temple, carried it in a huge ceremonial procession to the capital, and afterwards reburied it in the treasure-crypt. The crystal sarcophagus in turn contained a white jade reliquary in the shape of a coffin that held the actual finger bone during its journey.

LEFT:
Gilt silver reliquary in the shape of a casket depicting 45 Buddhas; the silver casket protected the crystal reliquary.

The crystal sarcophagus in turn contained a white jade reliquary in the shape of a coffin that held the actual finger bone. After the crypt was sealed in 874, it was not opened again until 1987.

ABOVE:
White jade reliquary in the shape of an inner coffin with a chamber door.

ABOVE:
The iron casket is the outermost of four nesting reliquaries.

FOLLOWING PAGES:
Set of four nesting reliquary boxes.

SELECT BIBLIOGRAPHY

Barbieri-Low, Anthony J. 2007. *Artisans in Early Imperial China*. Seattle: University of Washington Press.

Benn, Charles. 2002. *China's Golden Age: Everyday Life in the Tang Dynasty*. Oxford: Oxford University Press.

Cahill, Suzanne E. 2009. *The Lloyd Cotsen Study Collection of Chinese Bronze Mirrors, Volume I: Catalogue*. Los Angeles: Cotsen Occasional Press, Cotsen Institute of Archaeology Press, Monumenta Arcaheologica 25.

de Bary, William Theodore and Irene Bloom. 1999. *Sources of Chinese Tradition*, vol. 1, 2nd edition. New York: Columbia University Press.

Eckfeld, Tonia. 2005. *Imperial Tombs in Tang China, 618 – 907: The Politics of Paradise*. New York: Routledge Curzon.

Gernet, Jacques. 1982. *A History of Chinese Civilization*. Cambridge: Cambridge University Press.

Ledderose, Lothar. 2000. *Ten Thousand Things: Module and Mass Production in Chinese Art*. Princeton: Princeton University Press.

Lewis, Mark Edward. 2007. *The Early Chinese Empires: Qin and Han*. Cambridge, Mass.: Harvard University Press.

——. 2009. *China between Empires: The Northern and Southern Dynasties*. Cambridge, Mass.: Harvard University Press.

——. 2009. *China's Cosmopolitan Empire*. Cambridge, Mass.: Harvard University Press.

Loewe, Michael. 1968. *Everyday Life in Imperial China*. New York: Dorset Press

——. 1979. *Ways to Paradise: The Chinese Quest for Immortality*. London: George Allen & Unwin

——. 2005. *Faith, Reason, Myth, and Reason in Han China*. Indianapolis: Hackett Publishing Company

———. 2006. *The Government of the Qin and Han Empires*. Indianapolis: Hackett
  Publishing Company

Nylan, Michael, and Thomas A. Wilson. 2010. *The Lives of Confucius*. New York:
  Random House.

Paladan, Ann. 1998. *Chronicle of the Chinese Emperors: The Reign-by-Reign Record
of the*
  Rulers of Imperial China. New York: Thames and Hudson.

Rothschild, N. Harry. 2008. *Wu Zhao: China's Only Woman Emperor*.
  New York: Pearson.

Schafer, Edward H. 1963. *The Golden Peaches of Samarkand: A Study of T'ang
Exotics*.
  Berkeley: University of California Press

Steinhardt, Nancy Shatzman. 1990. *Chinese Imperial City Planning*. Honolulu:
  University of Hawai'i Press.

Waley, Arthur. 1989 *The Analects of Confucius*. New York: Vintage Books

Wang Zhongshu 王仲殊. 1982. *Han Civilization*. New Haven: Yale
  University Press.

Wright, Arthur. 1959. *Buddhism in Chinese History*. Stanford: Stanford
  University Press.

ACKNOWLEDGMENTS

Exhibition Planning: Peter C. Keller, Ph.D. and Anne Shih

Exhibition Management: Cultural Relics Bureau of Shaanxi Province and the State Administration of Cultural Heritage

Exhibition Lenders: Famen Temple Museum, Han Yangling Mausoleum Museum, Lin Yu County Museum, Museum of the Terra Cotta Warriors and Horses of Qin Shi Huang, Shaanxi Archaeology Institute, Shaanxi History Museum, the Xi'an Museum, Xianyang Museum , and the Xixiang County Museum.

Publication Sponsor: Resources Global Professionals

Guest Curator and Catalog Author: Suzanne E. Cahill

Contributions By: Albert E. Dien, Ph.D., pages 19 and 21

Curatorial Coordinator and Catalog Editor: Julie Perlin Lee

Publication Coordinator: Lesley Ann Hamilton-Keating and Victoria Zagarino

Catalog Copy Editor: Sue Henger

Graphics Coordinator: Nancy Ravenhall Johnson

Graphics Assistants: Sasha R. Contreas and Eleanor Harbison

Photographs: Courtesy of the Cultural Heritage Bureau of Shaanxi Province, Wang Da-Gang and Christine Johnson

Publication Design: Shanghai BBS

Designed by: Yao Weiyan, Bai Jinyi and Zhang Jingjing

Printed and Bound by: Shanghai BBS Art Design Co., Ltd.

Print Supervisors: C&C Joint Printing Co., (Shanghai) Ltd.